what to do

with

RED

what to do
with
RED

jacquelyn shah

Lit
Fest
Press

Copyright © 2018 jacquelyn shah

ISBN: 978-1-943170-27-2

Cover design courtesy of Zarina Shah

Interior Design: Jane L. Carman

Published by Lit Fest Press, Carman, 688 Knox Road 900 North, Gilson, Illinois 61436

Lit Fest Press

Outside the box

ACKNOWLEDGEMENTS

The following poems appeared in these journals, sometimes in a slightly different version and/or with a different title, as noted:

Tar River Poetry
"Dog Days"

Encodings
"Retiré, Exposé" [published as "Toe Shoes"]

NCASA Journal (National Coalition Against Sexual Assault)
"Look Out" [published as "One Good Arm"]

South Coast Poetry Journal
"Letter from K on a Drunken Raft"—Contest: honorable mention

The Cape Rock
"Sideshow"

Amelia
"What Masters Your Head"—Contest: second prize

It's All the Rage! anthology
"Staring" [published as "Staring from a Hood of Bone"]

The Texas Review
"Paul's Balls"

Margie
"Here's to Refraction, Uncle Fred"

Cranky
"Amalga Mates"
"Crazy Eights"

The New Zoo Poetry Review
"I Pledge Allegiance"

Anon (British journal)
"Perfect"

[com]motion (online journal from Small Wonder Foundation, California)
"Mickey's Pants"

Change Happens anthology
"Divertimento"
"Strange Garment"

Rhino
"—Q-self, Jading"

Vine Leaves Literary Journal
"Anger"
"Domestic Arts"

✦ FORTHCOMING ✦
Fiolet & Wing
"Still Life with Fruit, Froth & Kinesis"

I am thankful for my Individual Artist Grants from CACHH—the Cultural Arts Council of Houston and Harris County, and HAATX—Houston Arts Alliance; my grant from the Puffin Foundation; a Barthelme Fellowship for poetry and a travel fellowship for the Kraków, Poland Seminar, Jagiellonian University—both from the University of Houston.

I appreciate my writing locales: Barnes and Nobel–W. Gray, Houston; The Teahouse–Shepherd, Houston; coffee shop EQ Heights, Houston; Campesino Coffee House, Houston; various Starbuck's locations and sundry libraries in Houston and Cincinnati.

I celebrate Harwood Taylor, host of the Friday breakfast at "Harwood Cafe," where poets-artists-storytellers, friends and keen listeners—Chris, Mary Carol, Tacey, Michael, Jim, Naomi, Nicola, and inimitable dog, Clease ("enthusiasti-Clease") et al. gather for superb healthy food, tea, and hospitality.

I enjoyed and was grateful for (2009 to 2015): my renewed Cincinnati friendship with Bob Herrmann, classmate from kindergarten through 12th grade; my camaraderie, support, and feedback from members of the MMWG–Monday Morning Writers' Group, which still meets at Joseph-Beth Booksellers in Cincinnati.

A resounding thank-you! To Jane L. Carman at Lit Fest Press

TABLE OF CONTENTS

III. ANIMAL FORM

IV. WHAT MASTERS

HIATUS

V. SENSE & NONSENSE-ABILITY

ALL dedicated to ALL the women I know…
with special reference to Iris, Tanya, Zarina, Leslie, Stacy, Bevin, Susie
Trishala, Manjari, Roopa, Kim, Mary, Grace, Claire, Risë, Elline, Sehba
Anna, Lucie, Mica, Hazel, Laura, Debbie, Pam, Lilian, Denise, Janette, ET AL.
& my perspicacious Persian cat—nonpareil—Eliot Carson Roosevelt

Red is the share of fire
I have stolen
from root, hoof, fallen fruit.
Linda Hogan
"The History of Red"

I will not be clapped in a hood,
Nor a cage, nor alight upon wrist,
Now I have learnt to be proud
Hovering over the wood
In the broken mist
Or tumbling cloud.
William Butler Yeats
"The Hawk"

It is a serious thing
just to be alive
on this fresh morning
in this broken world.
Mary Oliver
"Red Bird"

PROEM

OPEN-AND-SHUT

I will not sit on a line
   like a noisy magpie
screeching my life into air
   I have a shut beak gleaming
squinch eye reflecting red,
    dark—my line of vision

Warming myself
   within a neat nest
I peck at the huge
   inscrutability outside—
the world's branched rot
   and emptiness

When I've swallowed enough
   beak instinctively opens
to pour out a chyme
   and lay it on the line

OBSESSSSION

O of it ringing me   wringing me   circling my iris-of-eye   circumscribing my I

Bang of it   bread-in-the-belly & buzz-in-the-head of it   beating & bleeding &
besting me

Squeeze of it   need for it   prodding me   kneading me   shot-in-the-arm for me

Eel of it   easter & christmas & squeal of it   evening & morning   moon &
mole of it Quious & quiddity   beleaguered bejeweled beholden

Sis-boom-bah-hotbed!   Sis-boom-bah-humbug!

Sis-boom-boxed roar of a secret magenta   lure of it   pure with it   luxed-&-
utopianed

Sisyphus pushing   sisyphus pushing   sis-sis-sis-sisyphus pushing & pushing &
pushing

Siren ball-peening-&-penning   seized-by re-seized-by the balls I don't have

I am the eager-&-eagle ply of it   mistress-&-child of it   rapt & peignoired in
it—the ur-*O!*

O*! O!* of knowledge & outrage   ripe overripe indignation   huckster
homespinning my I-as-a-

Nation of gr-r-r-&-indwell   encrypted   figured   nail-polished & narrow in fury
& calm

I. KNOWING

I like to make use of what I know.
Franz Kafka
The Trial

I KNOW
Any bird that knows its place in this world
can be quite content. Alfie Bill Naughton
A small bird I know my place I do
          Zbigniew Herbert, "A Small Bird"

Spreading spinning loving falling humming
          trembling   because of disobedience
                    leaving the tree   leafing a new tree
               rubbing bird-self on bird-self   watching the sparks

                                                  flash!

          within seared feathers and wings of ash
Spreading spinning loving falling humming
          trembling   to leave behind in the snake-ridden tree
                    any voice that would praise   tree and snakes
               any loving too much   with wet little feathers
                    any beak a little too sweet
Spreading spinning loving falling humming
          rambling   place to place   with no hope   of place
                    growing attached to the ramble   and having

                                                  no tree

     nesting in spaces   of bramble rock dust dolor
Spreading spinning loving falling humming
          beginning to think   of a voice   flying past moon
                    pecking the sun   hatching a song
Spreading spinning loving falling humming
          always spreading spinning loving falling humming always

                                                  bird

Woodcock: the essence of this strange little bird—
to be and do anything but what would
normally be expected. Its flight is erratic,
its brain is upside-down.

QUITE CONTENT

        to be a bird—but only woodcock
      through buttercups and irises I peck and *peent*
   knowing what I know, I spread
    my droppings far and wide
and know my places—where I've chirped
where I've dropped
dreamy in the strange
the ineluctable
the depths
of everything transparent, inexplicable   I peck
tuko peent   I peck and idle
peck and range
              through perwinkles   moss and leaf   rose and litter
  lovely places where I probe the soil, hearing
every churning of worms   watching, all the while in all
    directions: up down ahead behind side-to-side and inward
  with shiny shoe-button eyes
       for fox   snake   skunk   and scintillation

Content   solitary   seclusive
I live on the floors of thickets near violets
by vibrance iridescence dead leaves and golden drops
    lovely places where I shake my feathers, pecking
at spangle veil and cluster   while I cool my little bird-
  brain   render droppings on root and rot

HERCULEAN

Conquer a lion by first shaking him up
      then spearing his best parts

Digest as many heads as possible

Captivate one old bore

Infiltrate a stag party to learn what you can

Devastate all rapacious old birds

Remove your girdle to display
      an Amazonian girth

Cleanse the animus of one old king
      to stabilize his flow

Enchant one raging bull

Neutralize four young stallions

If need be, kiss a snake
      even as you walk with the cows

Bake an apple pie for one old dragon

Make one dog heel   heal one old dog
      dog one old heel

DOMESTIC ARTS

I.

Cut the zucchini and be content
  to cut what cannot bleed
make a line of discs a little spine
  clothe the spine in oil that won't
anoint   and sear sear sear...
  then thread and hang the thing
in vegetable effigy

II.

Circle round yourself and be
  content to fill yourself with self
take your cue in other words
  from men who've circled men
be loyal to yourself   dog-best-
  friend-wise   sit fire-side and smoke
for flames would only make you ash

III.

Use the smoke to darken walls
  your own   smear it   all around
drink to smoke and mirrors
  mirror what you see then write it
with a lipstick on your breath-
  fogged glass in cuneiform and rune
in your own room artifact it all

IV.

Cut on   cut on... happy with the cannot-
  bleed   internally make this kind
of sublimation force a sentence to
  the surface where a pock or two will run
a little   just enough to sully words
  too smooth   take satisfaction as you peel
the skin from carrots   dice and boil them

STILL LIFE WITH FRUIT, FROTH, & KINESIS

On a rosewood dining room table overflowing a lead-crystal bowl: hot tomato
apple kiwi lemon guava   cantaloupe sloped over grapefruit pissing off peach &
    pear
papaya   breadfruit starfruit jackfruit   date & durian   apricot banding with
kumquat   nectarine mango tangelo lime   pineapple pumpkin chin-upping cherries
berries black & blue & dew   huckle & goose & elder   rasp & straw & cran & bil
lichee licking a quince   grapes all peeled black-red-green   champagne & globe
honeydew water & crashaw melons   persimmon & plum perfecting themselves
tangerine plantain coconut currants   oranges, copious mandarin navel & blood
seeds squealing out from a fat pomegranate as raisins debate & debate the dubious
wonders of botox   figs & bananas bananas bananas-of-course a little green
worm is fucking the fruit—tomato apple   then kiwi lemon guava… all in the fog
of a grand starbuckian steamed-milk froth…

STILL LIFE WITH SNAKE, HEART, KEYHOLES, ERASURES, & SOMEWHAT PLAGIARIZED PLUMS

Like a long silk stocking left over from another age the snake has positioned itself
next to one heart's finest erasure (after peeping-toms at twelve keyholes wore out
their dancing shoebutton eyes & angel cake infestation attempted to foil all gangsters
though Democritus was not amused by the brouhaha when sly little plums said *hello,
we too are dissolving soap* as the snake hoped for a bit of clean beauty & eleven
very large erasures were starving themselves into zero tolerance for non-being
as ten slim gorging Indian Princesses relinquished apricot in favor of greengage
gowns &, too, the snake couldn't help but vote, regrettably, for nine erasures—
so, gone! Nine inaudible cries divided themselves—such hemisemidemiquaveries!
One remaining heart began to puke itself & how red is that, tit-tat? Snake, pit viper
to be exact, savored the jazz that was not being played through the silence of what
was still life… but suspiciously resembled an erasure)

PAUL'S BALLS

i am crying over the american male, he said, my tears fall thick and fast
because of golf, tennis, polo, jai alai, bowling, croquet, roulette, pool, boule,
billiards [et al]… the invention of the ball was a tragedy. it has led to centuries
of piddling. it is impossible to make the american male see the gross absurdity
of spending years chasing balls and catching balls, batting balls, slinging balls…

Philip Wylie, *Finley Wren*

Hell's bells—there they are again!
Paul's balls. Everywhere I look
they sprawl, two hollow fellows.
Marshmallows in my morning cocoa?
No, those damned Paul's balls.
In my toiletries among the cotton puffs?
Those balls. In my daughter's toy box?
Those balls. In the kitty litter box?
Those balls balls balls balls balls!

Billiards, anyone? There they are,
racked and ready to disperse.
Night sky with a pearly moon?
Sharing the high, those balls
those balls balls balls balls
          balls balls balls!

See the rolling of the balls round the globe
with Bunyan bulk   puffed and purplish
see the people they impoverish
with their claiming and declaiming
with their banging and their hanging
keeping score score score
in their ever-waging war
in their war war war war war!

Brake brake brake
the rolling of the balls, O Paul!
The controlling and patrolling of the balls.
Let the heavens start to twinkle with a crystalline delight
as we tame tame tame
with a kind of cosmic aim
the superannuation of the Pauls
transubstantiation of the balls balls balls
to the belles!

SNOWMAN'S EYES

Tradition: act of delivering, surrendering;
process of handing down; inherited
way of thinking; body of beliefs

nothing   surrendered
nothing   inherited
his way   of thinking
  not my way
his body   of beliefs
  not my body
his tradition   of snow
  my nothing   his snow
out of heat   no tradition
I write   of quiet fury
my vision   a pool
of water   I look at snow
see nothing   but cold
staring in   the snowman's
eyes I see   chips of coal
hard dark   my source of heat

TRISKAIDEKAPHILIA

13

Flying in from midnight only the beady eye
will have the beauty of thunder sung

13

Once there was a hat with thirteen ribbons
another hat with thirteen more, another, another...
and none were torn asunder

13

To be under the thirteen-ribbed umbrella
may shield you from the reign of a despot

13

Can you tell the two apart?
Thirteen guys come in from ruined fields
thirteen gone out to begin
enormous ruin again

13

Thirteen busy old fools of business and drool
racing around in a corporate playpen—
dismiss them, all thirteen

13

You must persevere.
   Boccaccio, born 1313
Always do what is right in whatever state you find yourself.
   St. Catherine of Bologna, born 1413
*Reading that pleases and profits, that together delights
and instructs, has all that one should desire.*
   Jacques Amyot, born 1513
No man is clever enough to know all the evil he does.
   François de la Rochefoucauld, born 1613
You have to make it happen.
   Denis Diderot, born 1713

Don't forget to love yourself.
    Soren Kierkegaard, born 1813
And what if the universe is not about us?
    May Swenson, born 1913
What will some wise one say,
    born in 2013?

            13
Count the tricks, count the kicks—
the numbers dwarf thirteen
            13
The sadness of all that's gone before
cut into thirteen strips and flung
way out to thirteen oblivious stars

            13
Accentuate the positive and maybe
you'll stay another thirteen days
here in this haven apart from the craven

            13
Prime number meaning purity
Thirteen moons in a calendar year

            13
Thirteen parts of the cut-up Osiris
was all that was found
A fourteenth, had been eaten by fish:
his penis

            13
When a Friday rolls around
and your beady eye worries itself
to a desolate state of un-thunder
count yourself lucky that you're immune
to paraskevidekatriaphobia

jacquelyn shah
33

13

O happy, happy number—thirteen
When your one is squared
and your three as well
your resulting ten is one
and zero
Each squared and added is one
That's me, prime one
who hails the smallest emirp

LETTER FROM K ON A DRUNKEN RAFT

Dear Charlie,
I write to you from Flux, the sea of a sea-
blue funk that flows through middle ages. I float
like Quetzlcoatl on a raft of snakes and flaunt
my malice and pique that rain on your jamboree.

I'm on my way, I'm on my way, I'm K.
Yet castles seem to fade to a check-point, Charlie—
your boot, your bluff, your global hurly-burly.
This floating's a helluva job, and what does it pay?

The Bald, the Bad, the Bold, the Fat and the Simple!
Sometimes a Wise, a Well-beloved, or a Great,
but I can't remember the deeds, the conquests, the fate
of a single Charles. Or if anyone had a dimple.

But they all came to my bedroom, every one.
I fêted them in all their coronations,
jollied myself through so many mutilations,
took every bloody kiss as sine qua non.

Great pretender, pumping iron on the throne,
you're a little tramp, Charlie, full of holes.
Charlie, you're vile, you stink of fleurs du mal,
and what could you know of real murder, my Chan?

You're a snake in Brown's clothing, egghead charm
the best disarming tactic. But I'll survive.
That kind of ruse can only feed my drive
to be among the fittest, dear old Charles.

I could modulate to a Larry, Moe, Curley,
but I'll sail to the true eye of this letter: life
(we used to sing back home in Cincinnati)
is just a bowl of Charlies—

                              signed, your wife.

SCREWED, BUT STILL HOPING

Worm went along, barely aware
　　of the screw in her side
Toad was trying in vain to un-
　　screw the one in her belly
Smelling a rat, Old Bat, nonetheless
　　rejected the truth of teeth & tail
while Dog, blind to the screwedness of Dogness
　　slavered, to no avail
She yanked at the screw in her flank
　　pert Pig, turning turning—no luck
Hot, red & let's-go-to-bedish, Tomato
　　trusted the screw was a *you*
Poor Chick was moppin' up blood
　　Screwed! tweeted Bird *All screwed!*
Hogwash! Old Cow countered, chewing a cud
　　No such thing! She twitched
her tail, luring gadflies, scads
　　That's when Bird knew
for sure, they were screwed Still
　　hoping—who knows for what?—
she bolted… then finally molted

SON NET: ELL... IPSO FACTO

> *... woman is defective and misbegotten, for the active*
> *force in the male seed tends to the production of a perfect*
> *likeness in the masculine sex; while the production of woman*
> *comes from defect in the active force or from some material*
> *indisposition, or even from some external influence; such as*
> *that of a south wind, which is moist...*
>
> Thomas Aquinas

Fact: from my ell I'm free to add   omit
dredge up whatever   or not   at will
because I am ill (-conceived [♀] -egitimate)
I never concern myself with being well
my privil (do not mistake for drivel) -ege
the finest *bene* fit that pundits have be-
queathed   unwittingly   gives me an edge
a chance to flit nitwittingly a bee
like one   most fittingly   in my *bon* net
with little taint of saint-inspired la-la kyries
my ipseity's   albeit relative   immaculate
and so... my best elimination frieze
a tempered   moist   & straight-from-the-net erasure:

plus this south-wind ending for good measure

GO WISH UPON YOURSELF

his story   her story   his story
her story   history herstory

      —who cares?

alternately bored & furious

this configuration

of cells   tissue   organs

this being being-me

wants to rise from the sad sod of gendered earth

shoot out as billions of blinks

assemble

over the flap

& hang

sidereal

above it all

wishing only *starlight starbright*
on my luminous self

II. MOCKYJABBER

Two tongues from the depths,
Alike only as a yellow cat and a green parrot are alike,
Fling their staccato tantalizations
Into a wildcat jabber
Over a gossamer web of unanswerables.
Carl Sandberg

PAW

It was when the big bear of a truth raised paw
  its shadow every bit as menacing
as hairy-clawed enigma of the endlessness
  and grotesquerie of strong-veined matter
It was when this bear forced consciousness
  slapped it into comprehension
that breakdown metamorphosed into break-
  away, and living in the shadow forced a way
of composing virgin habitat and realizing honey

It is when the word to paw is dripping, dripping
  and all sweetnesses seem endless, ordinary
when the oh-so-seemlinesses overarch and overbear
  that inner grizzle laughs down muzzle
and peach, all fuzzy, uses paw

DO YOU DARE

        disturb the marmalade, make a sudden leap
  & curl around the cold cold porcelain?
Go on… without a necktie
  with invidious intent to spread
& etherize eternal Footmen—Go
  away from yellow arguments to fog
& smoke malingerers with your snickering
  cawed ragging, scuttling,
however foolish, manialogue
  Oh, do not ask, *Why diss it?*—
nothing here's illicit

Go mutter all your bleatings
  with formulated phrases bent
like coffee spoons
  chipped like teacups
to be rubbed against the faces & the universe you meet
Lick every corner as you muddle & create
  Upon a yellow plate then drop
a little Michelangelop
  Inconsequential, impolitic, incautious? I grow old…

Ridiculous? To yellow eyes that fix you, sum you up
  as butt-end? (Should you assume?)
To flannel, flapping, rolled or squeezed
  into a ball? To fools hirsute or bald,
lonely, moving towards you, if at all,
  hardly subtle with their claws
Shine a magic lantern on them…

Warhorse on a sawhorse in your wilderness—go on
   sprinkle sawdust, soot & oyster-shells
over sentences a bit obtuse upon a platter
   Make one great splatter, don't be muzzled, this is it,
this bitten-
            off matter, chewed   rechewed & chewed—
it's exactly what you mean, each digression & aggression on the table
   Let your modest vision be this wriggling revision
adverted with a simple yellow pin, then…
   Leap! and fling them to the wind: caution
                         & a well-gnawed peach

PARADELLIAN

The paradelle originated in eleventh century France?
No. It is a parody of the villanelle, created by…

In spring my mockery calls itself blue.
In spring my mockery calls itself blue.
But what, I say, what about green?
But what, I say, what about green?
Calls itself green in my spring,
mockery? But blue, I say, about what what.

It is time to hold high the little parasol.
It is time to hold high the little parasol.
And bend another war-horse to one's will.
And bend another war-horse to one's will?
Will the war-horse hold another time?
It is one's little high to bend. To parallel and.

Over the river and through the woods we go.
Over the river and through the woods we go.
My right-left paradiddle knows the way.
My left-right paradiddle knows the way.
We go the river way through woods
over the left-right, and my paradiddle knows
[this going nowhere's not for long—you come too]

Spring? High time. Hold the woods
to parallel and paradiddle, left-right. I bend
the war-horse to my will, through my blue
way, and about. Over we go? One's little parasol
is in the river. Say, but mockery calls
another what? It knows, itself, the what—green,
this going. [Nowhere's not for long—you come too]

LEAFHOPPER BALLAD

In the grass, an insect
chewing with a zeal
ingesting do-dads by the yard
each one a treacle

To trip the switch of mouth was all
the hopper cared about
regurgitating hybrid chunks
from every eating-bout

And so… a song of chomp & passion
another one of doubt
lauding of the chewing motion
with chirrup   trill   knockabout

In love with malt & spit, it titivated
felt within the blood
electric surges of its might
about pure myrmidons of mud

Within the celebrated grass
that gave the insect food
for thought—a serpent
in a wicked mood

Sing you little insect soul
be poet of… blah   blah
Just so, it oozed its hopper-dew
oblivious to sneer

or scoff   shrug   sniff   So…
more tweak & twittering
more rivulets & rocking
out on the open road—

It loved its mouth with weed—
Blow my bugle me, it sang
o drum my self, go pound along!
With suck & burp & spit

and then more burp more spit
of *hopper hopper hopper*
until the snake ate...

TARZANNA

When swinging is the single solidarity to be found among the apes
        one goes looking for a sturdy vine
and courage to negotiate whatever gully cuts through comprehension.
        Tension is the key and culmination
once a foothold is established, even as ever-ugly ungulates undulate
        until you want to scream.
You may hate rodents, but making friends with capybaras is essential.
        Macaw macaw macaw and caw
of crow is all you'll hear and hear and hear, you bet.
        The thickset python will coil
given half a chance, and wrap and coil and wrap until
        your bones snap.
So keep on swinging as you clutch your knotty vine and pour
        a flute of vinegar on the villainous.
Your only proof will be in spoof, and dangle will be fitting
        for the jungle jumble of perdition.

ICE CREAM'S A MIGHTY FORTRESS

I

The emperor of ice cream floats & cups
in his hot little hand the souls of brussels sprouts
floats   unperturbed through downs & ups
but mostly ups   (don't count the drinking bouts)
the emperor of ice cream sandwiches
his core between the colds of arctic slush
premier so self-composed he never twitches
no gaffe no foot-in-mouth can make him blush
the emperor of ice cream sodas rolls
he does, a stone   and gathers no damp moss
what if he rumbles over cabbage souls?
So what? The emperor is boss
he's smooth he's cream he's right he drinks champagne
he's right he's ice & only drinks champagne

II

The emperor has set the trend & wears
a robe encrusted with a thousand gems
little winks & whines all snares
to trap the dupable   his stratagems
succeed   a fellowship of like-robed gents
purvey their this & that   the semaphores
of all that constitutes their wonderments
(they can even prove that they're progenitors)
perhaps there's something in the genes
that drives a lackey to the choir
of punks & dupes sheep & fellaheens
ice cream's a mighty fortress to admire
so do we all desire the robe & diadem
that we might feel ourselves as one of them?

III

Do all concur the emperor has no clothes?
(exposure cut from cloth of self to drape
the self in folds of self is nakedness
sublime) who sees the lack of shape
due to missing cartilage & bone
feet that pace in all directions all
too aimlessly   a tongue that speaks in tongues?
Who'll confess that he's been held in thrall
bamboozled by a rheumy pseudo-matter
(minus heart—not even one on sleeve)
& royal blood with all its mega-patter?
In ice cream truth electorates cannot believe
this rumtum prince is anything but
a dissolute brain rank with a prodigal gut

IV

In cedar-limbs he sat, the emperor   & smoked
a big cigar while singing wenches dithered
how cold   how dumb   the small & understroked
yeomen of yoghurt   tarred & feathered
tired, so tired   what's sour is forever
sour   play hearts lead spades & trump a son
span two continents & stuff your quiver
with arrows meant for someone on the run
a legacy is ready for the taking—
spoof or raise the roof   your office calls
true licks are sweeter than a johnny-caking
vaulting over peters   poaching pauls
look up & out   expand your jibe & josh—
melt that cream! exploit the all-aslosh

THE IMPORTANCE OF BEING ERNIE

Jack: Oh, that is nonsense!
Oscar Wilde

Ernie's at a garden party
ernie's in the country
Ernie's at a tavern
ernie's in the town

does a handstand on the grandstand
flies to urns & effigies
does a cartwheel into lust & thorns & trinkets
peels a worm depletes the hues
from worn-out rainbows & reverses
newborn elders

Ernie wears a gunny sack
ernie burrows in a haystack
shreds confetti winds bright neckties tight
around his own old weathered neck
& never scrapes the bottom

unless there's some wild goose to grasp
new moon-melt
molding into barely muffled grief
some trodden sod
to tamp down into brick-hard peat

Ernie does a tumble does a turn & bends
back flips back cra / cks a bone or two
& like the weed keeps tumbling & tumbling

Ernie ernie Ernie ernie—where
is the lullaby where the soother smoother
of too-crooked brows bring the sepals stamens

tendrils blooms for Ernie's rooms
ernie's in the orbit Ernie's in the sherbet
ernie-Ernie-ernie—wander through rocks
float around the maples catch a question
someone's waiting somewhere for your whistle
for your charm & amulet & dust

crowds are waiting for your dust
Ernie
waiting waiting
for your ernie, Ernie—
give them all vitality
with half an urn or so of august
triviality

VAN GOGH'S EARLOBE

Little lobe sailed off one night
in a wooden shoe on crystal light in sea of dew
a self so pale and soft
it's hiding now in roses
cool and white   in oleander pink
in spray of almond   gentle chestnut
a blink away from bandages

Off to vineyards   gardens   poppy-splash
parades of self and self and cypress
landing on a mountain in the springtime
it sits alone and broods
a field of irises comes sallying
each flapping head and twisted leaf
exuding velvet rage
a green with pointed frenzies
calling out for capture
sun-splayed centers roll their tongues, beseech—
   Taste me   taste me   feel me

nothing of this rapture stays within
the realm of single sense
little lobe grows eyes and fingertips
begins to throw a tongue in reverence
a nose to suck in all the livid sips of pulsing petals
spins itself from peak to peak to vibrate higher   higher

lobe goes sailing on the whorls of star grenades
dips its senses into every globe—olive pickers
Arles   Auvers   inmates   yellow   cornfield   yellow
reds declaim and blues are wild affairs
daub and swirl by ear and eye are rife
then it's closed to all but sun

fixation on the soon-to-sink
a fire-head that fails
can't outrun the shadows
darkness   swamp   mire   movement
through the soil along a river
seeds of light are sown
an unknown hand is scattering
a quiver   silence
swish again   like sand
seeds—tiny meat of possibility
yes, there *is* a tree   its flowers are red
there *is* the outline of humanity
in distance   roof and spire
faintest spread of life
nothing wilder now than waving wheatfield
nothing blacker than a crow-flap

A SWIFT KICK?
After Jonathan Swift
   "The Furniture of a Woman's Mind"

A pair of testicles, do note
is all the passion in his coat
He'll leap upon you in a minute
but understand there's nothing in it
All the credit he has claimed
for every virtue—*loyalty reason truth*—
he has named?
Ill-gotten inconceivable
Uncouth, the lout—think *torture murder war & rape*
   The very sound look import of words like these disrupt
   a mocking plaintive rhyme and rhythm… so much I stop
   pull away   pause
         reflect on *genocide*

Bandy-leggéd yahoo cuss!
The nerve to blaspheme us—
women he can't live without
repeat, can't *live* without

The furniture my mind has stored
however much deplored
is oak   maple   teak
                  not merely pique
made so well it will not wreak *real* vengeance
My foot was poised just so
aiming for… yes, just so
But stop, I said… *Who wants to see the fucker turn sea-green?*
No kick   I   am   Queen

DRIVING OFF SPLEEN

... a way I have of driving off the spleen... Whenever I find myself
growing grim about the mouth... high time to get to sea...
This is my substitute for pistol and ball.

                                        Herman Melville, *Moby Dick*

Call me calm   never mind my looming Thor
side   Thought I'd sail with no money in maritime
regions to water my world, a way to ignore
soggy November of soul & have a merry-old time
so no hippo gets the upper of me   I'll feed
on whales eels sea-hawks things that glide
or swoop to mind   what strangles   alarms   wolfweed
duckweed invading still waters   a pride
of lions jaundiced & harsh   With cunning I'll float
through wrecks alone   reach shore   break ground   step forth
with harpoon & harp   new harpy bearing skins—or rather
some blubber   Whatever I may get someone's goat
with a patch on my eye & compass in hand   It's north
for good sailing   or south east west   wherever... with blather

HALF-JIGGER SONNET ON THE ROCKS WITH A TWIST

... thou hast thy Will[y]
and Will[y] *to boot, and* Will[y] *in overplus...*
Shakespeare, Sonnet 135

The family jewels or balls or nuts or rocks
rich in jewels & nuts & such... blah blah
a bumper crop cornucopian crocks
    enough & more   of much ado & doodad doodah... .
drunk on baubles nuts & balls to boot
blotto   gewgaws balls nuts
    ditto—gewgaws nuts bull

CRAZY EIGHTS
  An Oulipian opus

Of Manageability's first Disorder & the Frustum
of that Forbidden Trehalose whose mortal tater
brought Débat into the Worry & all our wold
with loss of Eden till one greater Manageability
restore us & regain the blissful Sebum
sing Heavenly Musher & pursue things un-
attempted while brooding on the vast Abyss-
inian Banana & justifying Socks & Serpents

Oh there is blight in this gentle breviary
that blows from the green figures & from the clowns
& from the slang   it beats against my chekker
& seems half conscious of the jug it gives
O welcome métier! O welcome frisket!
now I am free   enfranchised & at large
may fix my hackles where I will

BE MEAN
After Pound & MacLeish

Nothing snew under the
Sunday Times waits for no
mandibles are called but few are
cheapened, two can live as
once is how many times opportunity
ox, and you shall receive
what snew¿ Pussycat. Expectedly

quite dumb, as an old swung-on thumb
in these jocko-at-the-top blown-off climes
true-blue   red-white   mute-fruit times
be wordless   motionless   below the sea
& expectedly be no-thing which cannot be
but mean as cat-shit   snot new—see?

III. ANIMAL FORM

BARNYARD-ME

Dum Cluks

When you wish upon a star
   makes no difference
how hopeful you are
   one chikin-shit wish
is a waste—
> *The sky is falling*
> *The sky is falling*
> *THE SKY IS FALLLLING!*

Wet-hen fury
   and a flurry
of let's talk turkey
   makes no difference
Nobody here but us chikkens
   dum chikans
clukking at deaf coks
   making no difference
NOT ANOTHER PEEP OUT OF YOU
      YOU YELL-O-BELLIED CHIKKUNS!
Mr. Jones has spoken.
O fly the coop! go on
   other wild-guse chaces
for your chickun-scratch
   to keep old henny-penny-pecking-
self clean, even in the dust

We We We

> *All the people like us are We*
> *And everyone else is They.*
>   Rudyard Kipling

We are having fun, someone says
another one wonders who is *we*
while the wheel goes round and round
What happened to the wished-on star

says wee wondering one, in sackcloth and ash
always down on a knee
always some kind of piggie *we*
wants more *whee*
but the greatest whee's reserved
for the few fat boars whose greed
is top-dog greed
and the wheel goes round and round

Scram Lamb

Without so much as a whispered *scram*
I was speaking very nicely
to little woolly lambkin
Nothing had happened
but the idea of shearing was germinating
and before I knew it, shears in hand
I was bending over poor little lamb-
self, which had lost my way
Your *baaa baaa* bleat's
not gonna cut it, I howled
No Bo-Peep on the horizon
little lost me was more lost
than I'd ever imagined self could be
Fleece white as snow, sure to go
wherever wolf-self went
lamb followed, to the school-
of-hard-knocks, about to lose her locks
She shuddered, I sheared, she shook
Making it clear she was lucky
to be skipping off
(sure to lose her nice-way again)
I trotted out my big-bad again
Woolly thing had scrammed
on her own accord
but soon I heard

a new tinkling bell
Howling, I reached for the shears
oh well

Cud

Culled verities
diverse and indigestible
make for a mulled-over
gummed wad
that can't be swallowed
No, this cow can't swallow it
Doomed to an eternity of chewing
days defined by grind and slurp
any old cow could hope to culminate
these longueurs of mastication
unbidden   But, no
With wet conglomerate
in pouched cheeks
this one alters
her slurping with carping
daubs then smears page after page
No amount of gnawing rage
can render cud fit
for even one stomach
She cannot stomach raw cud-truths
studded with horrors—
slash   rip   gash   blast
impending devastation, annihilation
global bull-crazy mayhem all around
This one cow who keeps cud
broods   aloof
chewing chewing chewing

STRANGE GARMENT

When the last fires will wave to me…
Then I will no longer
Find myself in life as in a strange garment
Surprised at the earth…
And the shamelessness of men

W. S. Merwin

I, the-real-true-whatever-that-is-I
don a donkey cape today
& bray bray bray
my loud hee-hawing
scarcely a ha-ha-ha-ing

Wide space of desert I live in keeps me
far from another like me
My bray drums alone in long ears, my own
which pick up curses too:
the ubiquitous *f-yous* from myriad jacks

But the nearly inedible's rich
& there's moisture enough from my chewing
to nourish a spirit of spewing, *hee-haw*
& formalize donkey splat, *hee-haw-haw*
Stubborn & born to be so, I'm donkey

today—my costume and poem are fitting
I may be donkey tomorrow… and donkey non-stop?
Strange how a cape can work
tropological wonders to ease the pack
of a jenny—one named, almost, *Jack*

ETERNITY WARD

In the pasture of the world,
I endlessly push aside the tall
grasses in search of the Ox.
   from verse 1 of 10 ox-searching
   verses by Kuòān Shīyuǎn, mister
   known as Chán master

Maternal, I'm endlessly pushing
to birth a new Ox, me a silver-pelted Fox—
sleek–hunted–tamed–chained
rabid & slavering

Ox   token for focus
Ox   a channel to Bliss
Ox   that endlessly pulls me, serene
through so many days of life
in a beast-ridden world—
   rats   snakes   sharks   skunks
   weasels   wolves   cocks
   badgers   boars & bores

Eternal, the need to gnaw
brain   nerve   gall
for sustenance
And whenever a scrunching is done
sweet new Ox carts me away

If I weren't a Fox
silver & clever
always musing on Ox
Screech Owl is what I'd be
Willful, though, I gekker
turn each incipient screech
to wily speech
as I hook to a cart my castrated Ox
that carries me off to Bliss

HENS & MEN

*Mr. Jones, of the Manor Farm, had locked the hen-houses
for the night, but was too drunk to remember
to shut the popholes.*

Animal Farm, George Orwell

Out of the pophole
   I clone myself
clone & clone & clone…
   until I'm a brood myself
as I brood on how I'd hone
   each BenKenLenHenry
to perfect the feathers of roosters
   that *of a feather* we might better
flock together, we hens & men

Out of the pophole
   I & my clones—
not one of us, not one of me
   a chick—will party & party
squawking & clucking
   but never drunk

We're hens & our party goes on & on
   never to end, as we try to emend
cock-a-doodles pernicious & feudal
   Not one of us, not one of me
shocked by the grievous & heinous
   is a hen without purpose & pen
who will peck-peck-peck-peck-peck
   peck-peck-peck-peck-peck, ad nauseam

BARKING FROM THREE THROATS

I.

I exhale the air of sense
each word meant to smell
like fir I swear you're not
a fire hydrant on which I lift
leg I'm your man's-best
friend devoted & a saint
bernard You insist the words
are barking raw like steak
but I only strain at the stake
to which I'm tied My underside
in shades of white & black
has furry good intentions coming

II.

from a wish to promote rapport
through use of lines
in catcher-uniforms determined
to enrapture readers who adore
the metaphor I conjure up a map
of underground aims & arm
myself with nets constructed
from furious phrases bent
out of busy barking
Heeling to syntax & hoping
the light in which you read is bright
I present this smooth surface

III.

surfeit of syllables in soliloquy
whose barks are ringed, scaly
fissured & totally figurative
With bark emergences sharp
& a tail of carp

I have brought all yap-words
out of inner moon-howl
through kennel of the kept
tug at your laundered pants-leg
& pant… in anticipation
of a future day of gnawing
one little old thrown bone

HALF & HALF

Sweet are the uses of adversity
Which, like the toad, ugly and venomous,
Wears yet a precious jewel in his head
                    Shakespeare, *As You Like It*

Adverse circumstances
this having no voice
not being heard
me, half Werneria—smalltongue toad
half bull
but the jewel's
thick skin and freedom

A stab will never find the soft
spot buried in a hide so tough
I'm free to spew
the poison of my warts

Head down   horns headed
for a target, I'm colorblind
don't see red
or white or black
A flap
of a cape
makes me hop
and a hop is a hope
since my quick little movement
sends me forward
and forward I am—
horning in on everything
I'll get where I'm going
as my sticky stubborn tongue
shoots right out

SHE WAS LAUREL

                    so what dogs peed
              all the way down to root
        with streams of sun-bright mead

By Mother Nature, spared Apollo's shoot
but what dogs peed
what mutts what pedigreeds
whose paw whose snoot
how many mangy breeds
what unseemly semen deeds
by Pug or Malamute
along with packs that peed & peed

May they go with Ganymede
to Zeus's root, whatever
dogs have peed
Scoot! Scram! Scat! Out—
damned Spot!

YAP

How do you know I'm mad?
You must be, or you wouldn't have come here.
  conversation between Alice & Cheshire Cat

Here   behind enemy lines   a naked tree
high as sequoia   your dog-self begins
its ascent   barking the slick trunk
with every conceivable trick
tapping along the way a sap   like liquid heart
its slight trickle enough for trouble   each bark
partakes in part of a brother bark yap of
old dog   reek of old dog your spoor
when toeholds are no-holds against a foe
        smooth as Spode   unforgiving   unbowed
you seek out nodes   gnarls in new bark
        to scale the trunk to a shudder of leaves
night in luxurious boughs with an owl
        a wood thrush and wind
                singing along with arboreal crickets
                        bathing in beams from a meteor
shower
your dog-self is sitting high on a branch
        after doggedly climbing   against the odds
                looking down on a field mouse, you smile
                        and then it begins—the old-dog
knee-jerk flap
                        like a Cheshire cat dissolving in reverse
                grin the first to go, you fade
        to bitch with nothing
        more than twitching
        tail   a common
        tale… but feet return   backbone   catface   grin

jacquelyn shah
75

SPORE

*A minute unicellular reproductive or resistant body
that is often adapted to survive unfavorable
environmental conditions and to produce a new
vegetative individual when these conditions alter.*

Like a wolverine, I grub in stink
    kick aside geezers & puff adders
twaddle that blinds me to maddogness
    bucking those who would ride me
to tame satisfaction   I feed
    like a condor on dead dogma
graze on sniveling voles   inviting lions
    into my web   I'm light
as dandelion hair
    tight as damask

Spitting out dry rot & mold
    I savor whatever I want
& make the rules in my forest
    furred & naked   finned & winged
I swim slither crawl walk soar
    in pursuit of glint
for a day I may rustle
    mayfly in the world's midnight
fire of firefly   darting searching
    for a vital orb in a galaxy clean distant
& ancient   I name my being
    with a single word

ANIMAL FIRM

I am A-N-I M A L
Chick Bird Hen Dog
Pig Shrew Cow Bat
I scratch peck paw root
suck chew butt flap
I am A-N-I M A L

Weird or wizened, wise as owl
with eyes wide open I see
in the night   feel the gloom
deplore the horror of world

My favored feathered form's
the Northern Mockingbird
I listen & sniff & mock
a lot   then mock & listen & sniff
My song will seem endless, I'm sure
for now it's endless, for sure

Preferred fur form is shrew
the venomous sort—look out!
for grooves in my spiky teeth

I am A-N-I M A L
brisk in any one mask
Fins are fine   rays are often right
Scales & shells will shield me
Horn   hump—both good for giving bump
in the treacherous night

Old bat with wings
& wringing hands
I am A-N-I M A L

IV. WHAT MASTERS

"Go away," says the stone.
"I'm shut tight."
Wisława Szymborska
"Conversation with a Stone"

WHAT MASTERS YOUR HEAD

What stays in your head is her head
studded with little unsprung snakes
pinned and pink-netted
her fingers nicotined a citric yellow
toenails long and talon-like.

What runs through your head is the dread
coming home from school, coming in from play
coming, always, to something coiled.

Standing in the kitchen, even then
you had a sense of the mockery of warmth:
waxed floor, baked cookies, red-checked cloth
daisyed apron. Anger.

Remember, though, the summer nights
kissing her at bedtime. But grudgingly
barely pressing the soft cheek flesh.
Still… feeling *something*. What rubs
in your head is regret.

You're glad you take your tea with milk
she drinks hers black.
Anything, anything that sets you
apart is pleasing. Anyway
one needs something or someone
to hate.   *Hate?*

She locked you out of the house
into the yard or cellar
for hours and hours.
Summer play in weeds and stones
cold, but glimmering stones;
winter skating on cement. Alone.

She cleaned laundered ironed cooked
day after day. Sat down alone
in the afternoon, to read and smoke.

Hate?
One night, very late
she had the courage to call a friend
spare you your father's drunken return.
What stays in your head is the rage—
theirs. And the long grind of bitterness,
hers. What tempers
remembrance is love, now...
of familiar repose, books and seclusion.

In your head is her raised hand, her head
writhing with snakes. What masters
your head is the stone, glimmering.

LOOK OUT

Sad flap   an empty sleeve
and his one arm raised
eyes squinting   mouth taunting—
a little boy named Jerry
in my backyard
                    You better look out...

It's mid-June   a few clusters of lilacs
still sweeten the air
but most have rusted
I rub my sweaty palms
in the pockets of seersucker shorts

I'm six   a little girl scared
of a boy behind bushes, a rock
in his one hand when I get off
the school bus   scared of one
arm and an empty sleeve

I hide my fear, carefully
like I hide my Hershey Kisses
left over from lunch
                    Yes, I look out...

ANGER

I've developed a taste for it
   savoring even mere scraps
like sweetmeats lodged in the teeth
   licks of cream that linger
I don't dress for the dining
   it's no formal affair
never a breakfast, no fast to break
  my gorging like my breathing's
steadfast   a bevy, my body
   of food vacuoles
a glutton for it, my belly's
   always growling lucky addict
I have fixes for a lifetime
   grow strains in petri dishes
delirious like a Frankenstein
   I fashion it   patch those saprogenic
memories, monsters, together—
   O sweet Elizabeth, the *too dear* sister!
In the night I grope for it
   lay with it, my skin crawling with it
like a memory-driven piston
   I'm drilling drilling
It's holy eucharist!   I sing hosannas
   scarlet letter stuck to my habit
bulimic, I spew fury   molten & common
   as cola   obsidian fact of life—*look at me!*
a skull & cross-boned bottle
   force no tonic down me   I don't want a cure
besides, it's powerful—my gag reflex

RETIRÉ, EXPOSÉ

The satin's scuffed, a whorl of worn ribbons
is dangling shoes from the closet knob. Dreams
have hardened into artifacts. As robins
usher in the spring, so do extremes
escort awakening. She used to dance
en pointe, in lace and tulle, her pageboy swept
and pinned to a smooth chignon. This elegance
was new to me (graceless, stiff, inept).
I watched *plié, tombé,* and *pas de bourrée
couru,* wearing tutu and leotard
self-consciously, mumbling words: *jété
développé.* Development was hard…
she serves canapés, as I expose
the bloody truth of ballerinas' toes.

SIDESHOW

Without a squeak
      they move to the big top
and back each day
      to their rare spectacle:
houses, huge, impeccable.

People painted bright
      oiled just right
who never eke livings
      just wallow
like Circe's hogs
      in fogs of enchantment.

Fresh from the spa
      women are not bearded, fat.
Even their moles have been
      removed. Men

don't have to swallow
      flames or swords
they eschew tattoos
      snakes don't coil
round them. Not a freak
      or a dwarf among them,

they are removed
      from the main arena.

BLUE GLOW

        —sounds like a prom in the 50's
low lights   mirrored ball
colors flickering
strapless gowns of tulle
clean collars and after-shave

Blue glow
       Omega Site   Pajarito Canyon
Blue glow
       plutonium   beryllium sphere
Blue glow...

       gamma and neutron rays...
Eight men rushed out of the laboratory...
drove themselves to Los Alamos Hospital...
Doctors watched the steady concurrent rise and fall
of the victims' blood counts...
as the radiation ran its course through their bodies

Victims?
Men with the capacity
determination
desire
for *blue glow?*

WHAT TO DO WITH RED
All nations striving strong to make red war yet redder.
Thomas Hardy, "Channel Firing"

Sweating my way to a giant red that's redder
than streets through a country redder than Emerald
City is green   without a drop of blood
without a drop of blood in sweat that bleeds one
corrugated way   peeled & julienned   baked red   red bread
boiling   potboiling over the stove   through varsity red-letter red
of burnt ears & faces lit   fox & fulmination
fast cars   spare ribs   engines & lights
Firing a lobster stream of lip-red   tulip-red & fever-
scarlet of tomorrow may not be another day
all the way to one great new morning sun that blisters my mouth

Arrow of fury through false red of false hearts
close at hand I keep that sun
for times when moon-self is sucked in on itself
left limp
like a pale useless lung

Gathering new reds clean as zinnias
ready for life
pyromaniacal   I buff   bellow   blow them
into curdling obesities
until their stretch-marks spread like wicked grins
& when I know I've readied them enough they're fit for war—

I poke!
They pop!

Like balloons rubber-flapping down   down   down
they slap the wet red bed of new tongue
where they poise, sadly
for re-inflation

MS. COSMETICO, WITH LIPSTICK

Let your helpless Anger be like the sea…
    let your sister Scorn not leave you
        Zbigniew Herbert, "The Envoy of Mr. Cogito"

Ms. Cosmetico daubs the lids
of your fiery eyes   stubbled jowls
snout   jaw   greedy claw
   with lipstick

Ms. Cosmetico crosses the T
of your furrowed-brow with a bindi
smears both poor-hearing ears
    with lipstick

She covers your pocked pimpled
adam's-appled neck & unheeding
un-hirsutulous head
   with lipstick

That newly rubicund head
resumes prodigious rumination
(looks, though
   like fussbudgeting)

With lipstick in hand
without a thought
Ms. Cosmetico mutters
                    Next…

SPHINX AND THE RIDDLES OF RED

She is Sphinx, ensconced on a desert floor
where picked-clean bones form a backyard heap.
I sit on stone, alert but helpless
clutching my own flaming *why*.

She is Sphinx enthroned and ruled
by her notions of probing.
The sun is rabid
nighttime bangs on our body.
Every new dawn is another
mean punch, times are bad,
morning worst of all. We wake
hungry—I for hope, she for a clerk
or a king, blind man, priest, judge.

When guesses come, she grabs them,
looking for an Œdipus who understands.
But that would be, I know
she knows, no one.

Imperial with knowledge, she's queen
in our desert space, gluts herself on diplomats
thanking no one for nobles who fall before her
plagued by her riddles of red. Her mouth
she wipes on monogrammed linen
purloined from moneyed questers…
while I sit and dream. Dream
of silver-winged feet
and galaxies green, but faraway.

Questions, hard and scarlet: our chewy bread and butter.
A garden of riddles is all we have, and all we give.

She is Sphinx, redness inscribes her.
I am Sphinx, crouched on stone
ruled by my probing
of red in her stony head.

KNIT PURL

Particle epistle physics: persnickety Gargantua. Inordinate
paroxysms of flux to weave the swatch.
Charles Bernstein

skein desk skip risk shape
sheikh dash shoot mesh spoof
spree asp speak lisp squeak
quick cheque quirk claque chirp
cheek stitch chain search plaint
pliant ripple plaited purple supple
suppose catsup superb gossip simple
ample jetsam amble dithyramb flimflam
flippant baffle flapper gadfly gatsby
gadget egad gadzooks baghdad baggage
bagatelle baobab babylon knitting-bag galahad
galvanize prodigal galavant madrigal marigold
manifold minuteman mandarin journeyman folderol
barcarolle cinnabar BARTLEBY zanzibar marzipan
mercury isomer merriment gossamer herringbone
ringlet daring ringlead luring ringside sideshow
bowtie rainbow bogus hobo ocher
curvy recur curly bon coeur sucker
sackbut knapsack sackful ransack suckle
tickle baltic ticktack mystic techie
quay yen knee zen zig-
zag craze zip jazz ze-
nith spin knit spun pun
punk kink puck dunk skin
scheme kitsch schiz desk skein

STARING

The woman is perfected.
Her dead...

Sylvia Plath

From a library shelf
I took the book and read:
Suicide, February 11, 1963

From desire to deed—
I tried
failed

Now when belly-up floaters in the head
bully with their neons and loose fins
burbling *die*
only my own sweet silver tongue
can talk the way to a great rebellion
as my hand begins to sculpt from bone
a day... another... another...

Years of living have made this mule-self-me
a champion   I do it well
It feels real   sometimes
I've sucked up
my own last tear
staring down the grim
the reaper

Alive, a woman is perfected
In a hood of bone she's equal to the staring
Dying's not an art
it's living that needs a gifted hand

HERE'S TO REFRACTION, UNCLE FRED

It's not as though I didn't notice your heart   after all
you made it clear when you unshirted your chest   made me press
my nose against the glass   all beveled & windexed
I thought *oh*
if only I could touch that meat-fist I could almost smell
(making me feel again
the joy of backyard grilling)   A sucker
for anything red and spasmic   I'm easily fed
I thought *ah*   looks like a moose ball   wanted to roll it
into my sweaty palm   You advertised it
as a two-for-one   deluxe and guaranteed   I lay
my cheek as you insisted   against cool casing
pretending that cloistered rouge-pot wanted to give of itself
imagining how rosy-glowed I'd be then   like a dawn
on the dance floor of you   how we might two-or-three-step
into midnight's favorite fog in tux
& boutonniere   slinky sequined dress & orchid
I had an image of it riding on the backseat   leather   of a Lexus
—RX300   3-litre V6   24-valve engine   intelligent variable valve
timing   automatic with sequential shift   Suddenly
I thought   I'll write a little poem to praise it
as though it were a fat angel in a scarlet gown
a chain purse full of peppermints   hot placenta stew
You raised my head   held my hair with one hand   pointed
with the other   I saw one red cent   a port-wine stain   a lobster claw
looked again   a bulgy circus nose   veiny scabrous nose   a wattle
chigger   chili dog   bloody gauze   a blotch   a nipple   jello jerky Spam—*Uncle!*
I jerked… you let me go… my heart was pounding… I thought *ugh*…
passed out & dreamed of gladiolas   poplars   thunder   courage…

GOT-NO-BLUES KINDA BLUES

No baby left me on the cold tin roof
No mama dumped me in the basin street
I'm singin' no-Saint-stuck-me   no-Louis no-kinda-blues

No peelin' those-potatoes slicin' those-tomatoes
liftin' up those garbage can blues kinda blues
No lady   no lady come rain or shine
Not gonna sing the cried for you, I got it bad
and that ain't good stormy weather blues

No gee baby   lover man   tin pan alley
what's new   St. James kinda blues
No fillet of sole   jelly roll
bless my soul blues

Nobody's dame   don't play that game
Got no cry a river or cryin' shame blues
No boogie   woogie   worried   weary
Wabash blues

Don't scoop up the moon unbutton the sun
leave north south west where they are
What's risin' in the east is... no cigar

My red scarf matches my eyes
I close my cover before striking
Not lovin' you not lovin' you I dine alone
but I won't be bananas

Got no blues no kinda blues
Enough said—no blues...
but boy do I sing red!

DIVERSE UNREST: A FERSKEYTLA

Having read the global red
realms untouched by prayer,
future bleak, I crawl into bed,
bank on NightBear-

nightmares clawing into calm,
coming armed with red
(reverse of bidden balm),
burning through my head.

Could I dream, instead, of ice?
Island where the people
work, sleep, play in peace,
place devoid of awful

red? Where harmony's a habit;
health prevails in mind,
body; neither dolt nor despot
dares to undermine

justice, equity; and each
emotion's sane. And yet...
white commands. What breach,
warfare, rape or threat

might devise disunity?
What delinquent rhyme—
order, meter, non-alliterate
line, length—disrupt this strict
verse? And spawn (perverse) revolt,
disorder, unrest?

jacquelyn shah

HIATUS

O FOR AN ODE!
... we opened two halves of a miracle...
            Pablo Neruda, "Ode to the Lemon"

If only he were here to praise me
            as the world's greatest eater
of red   here in this ruddy world
            I eat my mighty red
regurgitate and spread it

I would praise him for his salt
            the bite of which I take
from mine and cellar
            desert and sea
All I can sing is salt, which itself
            sings, as he says
in *moan* and *broken voice*

There's red   there's salt
            but I long to be cooled in lemon
deep in the glow of its *O!*
            If only I could write an ode
be subject of an ode
            —praise and be praised—
sweet open symmetry, no acid
            two halves of a miracle

V. SENSE & NONSENSE-ABILITY

Forgive me my nonsense, as I also forgive
the nonsense of those that think they talk sense.
Robert Frost

ARS POETICA-HA-HA

Backwardly, I grabbed it back
my poem, ha-ha, my brat
I promise you, I told it, another incarnation
if you will only kneel   assume the lotus asana
simplify an apologia pro vita sua
I'll give you something lighter   sweeter—

                                                        Sita

—if you find your necessary mittens
pull them over those intrepid paws
then you might have some pie   go up in a swing
ever so high   and say in truth   the play's the thing
*   *   *   *

My poem is a playground with no straight slide
swing-seats eight feet above ground and go-round
that's merry and more   a sandbox of *and*
a tip of seesaw towards *see*   it's jungle of jim
billy and bully and bob playing hob
see, it's not the pin but the juggling   not pick-up
sticks but picking up   my poem is the flying, and flying sand
when a dunebuggy eats up the beach
when it's sleeping you can steal an eyelash
drink the flush of its cheek and prattle
you can put it in a blue guitar and hear it
rattle   see it blush beside the white chickens
*   *   *   *

My poem is a monkey and dedicates itself
to Hanumaan and monkey's business: cracking
up   loyalty   love and the letter D   it's Durga
beyond reach   riding a tiger   eight hands curving
waving to its subjects: commotion   kaleidoscopes
antics and semantics   folly and Kali and crooks
it's both Shiva and Parvati   half male   half female—
Ardhanariswara   its female side
in low-slung bells and too-short T
is showing half a naval   half a crack   as it bends

it's a hobbledehoy   a Raggedy Ann/dy
can't sit up straight   think straight   in a world that's cracked
so it stays in its crooked (where the male is a kidding-aside
kind of jester) little piles   wearing, at best   crooked little smiles
without any cap   without any bells or cowrie shells
*   *   *   *

My poem is going to Knife-and-Fork Land
it's been hobbling in wastelands all too long
if it hurries it can sip a honeydew and stab
a slab of buffalo   as it rides the range in its mask
while it roams   it's a dear but it has no home
no envelope—just letter after letter and the west wind
is its postman and the least wind blows it east
and the wind, at last, is much of its feast
moveable, the poem will find a pieman somewhere
in the amber waves   buy his fare at the vanity-insanity fair
*   *   *   *

Along the way my poem met Simple Simon—it was the ides
of January—*hop on one foot   swing arms   all eight* he said
*follow me   I'm the pied piper   solitary reaper   appleseed Johnny
gnome on a broomstick   pod of the milkweed   Nod
from Wynken and Blynken land*   he stole
an eyelash from my poem   he said *jump,* and the poem—
a-mused till now—replied, *how high*   then ran away
with the evil-eyed chewed-on spoon and they both jumped
over the sifting shifting dunes   a-men
*   *   *   *

Here in my Woolf Room   lonewolf room   anywords-go-room
where the poem is a north wind (eating its high-fat cookie)
it can scrawl *soul swirl* even *twilight* with impunity
it says to itself, chewed-on old chum-chee, you can sprawl
—but do it with a smile, albeit crooked—nothing's straight
in this harlequinade   so hoist yourself up on a hobby horse
and lope through the nubs nudging up through the crumbs
*   *   *   *

My poem nailed a whalebone to its door and stuck a rib
from Adam in its pocket as it placed a Buddha
on its brannigan   a Pagliacci on the windowsill
it sat at home and wove a negligee by night
unraveled it at dawn   cut a wedge of apple pie
served it up with lace and arse-
nic   toothpick-stuck with a starry-eyed flag
it learned its lore from almanacs and comics
it waits for the dark of the moon to plant
rough old Trigger   it looks for its hour to come
it waits   and waits   for silver of moon to reap
*   *   *   *

Have you any penny, said the pieman
indeed, I haven't any, said the poem
so it went right off to make a deal   came back
with styrofoam from many a meal   crabbed machines
mounds of butts and chicken bones
and old rubber tires—too many, too many—
no one swings on a tire any more and a poem can only
eat up so many…
*   *   *   *

It won't behave—my poem might have to walk the plank
lotus feet scuffing along   dragging a ball and chain

It might get strapped to a chair   find its head
in a noose (blue-flowered, of course)

Its choices are all of the Hobson kind
it may suffer from dropsy and drool

It may suffer fools gladly   or not
when a willow is weeping it weeps   or not

If a nightingale sings it is thrilled   or not
its not is a maybe   its never is sometimes

It covers its face in a burqa, in order
to laugh   my poem must tickle itself

to last   cure itself with brine and smoke
pickle itself and burrow in hopes

The plank and the chair and the noose
are woodburned   embroidered   and woven

with leaves as green as an envy
flowers as blue as balls   on the beach
*   *   *   *

Simon said, *Poem, you mustn't wear*
yourself and he gave my poem an apricot
gave it both a crescent and a pasture
pulled from his trailing purple sleeve
he pinned a partridge on its bonnet
wrapped a lilypad around its adam's apple
and dampening a handkerchief
cleaned the corners of its mouth
He whispered something chastening
set it in a dirigible   waved winked... and let it go—

ARS POETIQUETTE
Derived from Emily Post etiquette

Never wear gloves
white or otherwise
during lunar lyricizings
always dress down
for the man-in-the-moon
that fickle S-O-B
When lifting weighty topics don't avoid
excessive grunting hissing huffing
Do not bow shake salute
but you can tip your hat and show your empty
hand—you mean no harm
Whenever you reach a famed fork
in the road, use the less-traveled & tuck
a napkin in your mouth if you're inclined
to spill your guts
Never dim headlights
as another poem approaches
from an opposite point of view—
and please! No pleasant tones—
insolence should be the rule
Show as much as possible
ankle, that is, as you elbow your way
through fragments of masters—
relegate nothing to margins but strew
the delicately lifted-out
through all your stanzas
with just a soupçon of guffawables
Display yourself not
on flowered paper but on heavy cream
marked up with black-eye ink
Fan-like, open and close yourself several times
to signal: *You're so cruel!*

Chew with open mouth while chattering
and always interrupt
A supple verse will sneeze in every face
scratch its head   pick its teeth   burp   spit and break…
wind down, then stop without apology

RIDDLING IN BEDLAM

Two chums were happy to meet in bedlam
for the purpose of ruining every euphoric palm.
Their desire to flesh out the story of rubicund cuckoos
matched their peculiar avidity for hairless people.
You know, the ones wearing jodhpurs, those who pretend
to shave heads, which are bald. They have their reasons.

Tangles of talk-about trails play havoc with reason
when precocious children decry the exhibits of bedlam—
live ones rather than wax. Speaking of cats who pretend
that a pack of liars doesn't tick on, from dust-motes to palms,
elucidation is more like a bell of alarm for all people
who just disappear down a tunnel as some cuckoo

announces the hour. Electric colors will cuckold
pastels, and damsels will injure their ankles for no reason,
jumping into the path of ice and its pebble.
I am available too, entranced by a bed where the lamb
interrupts one's counting of sheep. Thank the palm
for the rim of its skin where kind corners pretend

they are straight. Who in the creek can portend
the normal protagonists will smooth out kerchoos
and their bless-you's? The faithless. What's a date palm?
Dignified tree a-bristle with little-guy fronds. Reason
breaks down the deal between bladder and blanket. Bedlam!
A capitalist system is nothing but destiny's people,

nothing but rummaging millions of brash and cordless people.
Solution? Superior caution? The kiss and the mold will pretend
they're not on your cheek. Your bed's on the lam,
absconding with all your dreams of so-moody cuckoos.
Oh, well. Enormous green mounds have nothing but reason
when dementia runs its rapture to blur the vultures in palms.

Hey look! There's a penny and a rubber in your palm,
a taste of swill and flounder for all crazy people—
open wide! A smoky little valentine with devil's reason
will infest the truth until your dying moment. Pretense
will never breed an otherwise, no matter how the cuckoo
pops its head through pandemonium of escrowed bedlam.

People pretend the proximity of separate carnivals
is inconceivable, as cuckoos furtively palm a myriad of notes.
Bedlam has its reason, moat of riddles needling riddles.

BROKEN JAW: A CENTO

Little by little the idea of the true way returned to me.
I think I did right to go out alone—
but salvation here? What about the rattle of sticks,
stasis in darkness?
As a dare-gale skylark scanted in a dull cage
I twist last year into a knot of old headlines
and break onetwothreefourfive pigeonsjustlikethat.
This is the Sovereign Anguish!
This broken jaw of our lost kingdoms,
which cannot be imposed on the unwilling victim,
parched my yearning, and a tuft of cellophane
broke into brand new things.
So I say to the worm, Hey, Puke Head, you're wearing my
shed snakeskin in the history of politeness.
O for a beaker full of the warm South
and her teacup full of dark brown tears.
With those clear drops, which start like sacred dew
I have gone out, a possessed witch,
my heart in passion, and my head on rhymes.
Before me lies a mass of shapeless days.
They set up a noise like crickets,
turning modest lodging into wraparound tropics.
I remember the quick, nervous bird of your love
always perched on the thinnest highest branch.
I believe reality is approximately 65% if.
With ribbons and bibbons on every side,
and the too much of my speaking.

BROOMTIDE

O whither, o whither, o whither so high?
To sweep the cobwebs from the sky
And I'll be with you by-and-by.
Mother Goose

With a whisk and a wink into the ether of exactitude Wo-belly went sweeping low cobs
& webs of savage delirium out of the way, soaring into uncommon regions
sating itself on facets of starshinery on that plain Tuesday in its simple autumn.
Early into the moist midnight it was clear that success would be spelled S-T-I-L-T-S-
K-I-N and rumpling would be the end to all means. Simmering in one lacquered cauldron
then—new—a stew, spiced, herbed and served with a dice of garden-fresh weeds.
Glorious! the banquet-to-be. Countless tables were set and the goblet-happy crowd
began tucking napkins under whiskered double chins, cheery, hungry, unsuspecting.
Jesters frolicked! Three-legged dogs danced! And the Docent of Treason, Wo-belly itself,
licked fingers, lapping every squirt of wish-wine…then everything failed. Everything hanged
itself. Such dangling had never been seen. The after-feast, surprisingly, was more than enough.
Simmering stewing rumpling herbing and potpourri-ing—these ensuing doings were fine
even better than banquets. And better got better. Wo-belly dropped its meager woe,
pleased to become just Belly, brooming its way through disparate blimps and blotches,
sporting a never-to-be-deciphered new name—Mother Z—through all zones of
fiasco and famine. *Whither, o whither?* Up here high,

high above the despicable,

all too inexplicable fray.

ARUBA

I wasn't here so I couldn't take myself to that spot
over there where you could never be—
instead, I began to formulate someone who could go
to the other side of wherever the anyone's break
could be unbroken and to strive among all that's never
been tried in order that I might become a reliever
since I've never believed in a particular belief system
but have sung more than one or two praises of relieving
when getting out from under the multiple donkey burdens
assigned to so many of us that we can hardly see the beyond
that inevitably lies beneath a miasmic swamp called the benighted
mates of singulars that cannot see for all that darkness—
which, by the way, I have relegated to the regions of never-
go-there—when getting out from under propels you on a path
of bending & skirting & wading through bilge & dodging
airborne discards & elbowing your jagged way through mirages
carefully constructed to seduce as many potential collectors
as possible so that you come upon, pray come upon, appropriate
mindsets, which you too might like, since after all, though they are
probably not to your taste if your taste is less developed
than it would otherwise be had you continued your formal education
in the—I've forgotten what the major was—doesn't matter, since taste
is immaterial when it comes to discovering any regions that even resemble
the verboten remotely, but let it be known that anyone so demoted
as to find a place on the outskirts after bumped out of a good job
is routinely tethered to, to be sure, a major stick-in-the-mud
here-we-go-round-the-mulberry sort of futile and inane vision
and I would advise anyone to refrain from sneezing at my crap-shooter
relief system, which—ouch!—I'm feeling it again… so best I take leave
of the other side and get back to something less concrete, even if it means
attenuation or Aruba

BEDTIME, CUSHY PILLOWS

I am a servant of two masters—
Master Me and Master Me-two
They raddled and knotted
to get to this persiflage and set of balls

the cagey likewise of bedeviled winking
born of forty winks, among other circumstances—
treading hissing hurting—
as a life was constructed out of diamond-tears
and singularities barely chunked from tattered twilight
stories, in which the bread smells heavenly
One hired stormbird came bristling along
but anticipated that humdrumest blues
would overcook the tartest gumball
though it hardly mattered

since there would not be words for what are merely letters
to devise a truth   One spider will be standing still
(the past rain has already left) while others trap
bubbles in the makeshift windows of their edens
Someone in the jonquil speaks a stranger wine
hatched from the dream of leaving

such a shaky kakistocracy—an old story, sure
Crevices in some spinal sacrifice make wiggling endless
For all it's worth, keep following the gist into this ethos
where nothing of it will jinx the rats and cover your tracks
The sphere of reflections is two-dimensional—it has its ups
and downs   Silence is the outcome of long-term sputtering

Silence angels up the way to pieces of a peace

LESS, FOR THE PLEASURE
  After E. M. Cioran
  (and Basho, Wordsworth,
  Dickinson, Milton, Shelley)

In a work of psychiatry, only the patients' remarks
interest me; in a work of criticism, only the quotations.
  Old ponderer quotes
  nothing   leapfrogs over blooms
  pools a vain slobber

I have never taken myself for a being. A non-citizen,
a marginal type, a nothing who exists only by the excess,
by the superabundance of his nothingness.
  The moon in Spring in
  winter Rose in Summer   me
  this moment—nothing

Unmaking, decreating, is the only task man may
take upon himself, if he aspires, as everything
suggests, to distinguish himself from the Creator.
  Wander lonely with
  NO in host of golden Daff-
  ~~odils~~ until bliss fills heart

No difference between being and non-being,
if we apprehend them with the same intensity.
  Beady-eyed Shrike, me
  on narrow fellows in grass
  Same eyes on Zero

Not one moment when I have not been
conscious of being outside Paradise.
  Moments of gray—no
  Orchid or Chrysanthemum
  but Rose, out of chaos

I do nothing, granted. But I see the hours pass
—which is better than trying to fill them.
   Me lone and silent
   hours passing by in weird Wind
   —make serious sound? No

Sometimes I wish I were a cannibal—
less for the pleasure of eating someone
than for the pleasure of vomiting him.
   Pink Blossom on chest—
   gobbets of chewed Frog-Prince legs
   shoelaces soggy

What I know at sixty, I knew as well at twenty.
Forty years of a long, a superfluous, labor of verification.
   On edge of pool, young
   cattail   middle ripples   plums
   my own cool pond scum

No meditation without a tendency to repetitiveness.
   Old pond new jump   Splash!
   Splash-croak splash-croak croak-croak-laugh!
   No-frog leaps in daff ~~odils~~

AMALGA MATES

The Fully Developed Old Bat:
smooth rabid wooden club
tapered to a knob
equipped with wings & sharp
teeth   having a long history
of both fly-balls & home-runs
(during which much battering
diurnal & nocturnal takes place)

Tank:
large artificial receptacle
holding water & strictly
cold-blooded beings
mounted with cannon & moving
due to excellent mobility
cross-country (diurnally &
nocturnally) capable of shock action

Legerdemaintenance:
slight continual caring
by hand of the sleigh
its T having abandoned it
& disappeared—but who cares?
see   the caring has disappeared
but a slight nocturnal movement
of the hand & it's back

Worshipwreck:
at the bottom of the see mid sea-
weed & sand where eels lie
dying & the hull is splintered
a mermaid kneeless cannot kneel
& therefore does not praise the wreck
diurnally & nocturnally does not praise

HOLES

The potion drunk, spell begun, every last smile was gone. Not one to be seen. Even the lips, smirking or not, were shrinking, leaving nothing but holes, holes taking in, in and in, as much, much as possible, taking in everything, anything, stuff going in, going in to build great mounds down a ways from the holes, each mound wowing a torso. Or so it would seem. Holes from which poured a single word, over and over the sound coming out, ugly sound of an ugly word, with many repeats, rat-a-tat rat-a-tat style. Where had the other words gone? did they drown in a sea of stuff, crash on piles of stuff, or fade into thinning air? Or did they simply sink, sink into themselves? Little sinkholes, departure of words. Soon even the memory will fade. Memory of smile will fade, the era begin, Era of Holes, with the crowning of king and queen. King Hole and Queen Hole, lots of little holes coming, and so much sucking, sucking, sucking in, and in, so much sinking in. Potion-drunk, reeling and squalling and sucking, Holes, and Mounds, in a Capital Ship.

DRECKLINES

Give me your tired, your poor, your restless and your yearning–and I'll give them right back to you, barked Button-Down, bouncing from his Bimmer. *Have I got a deal for you*, countered Pinstripes. Later, over Grey Goose martinis, dirty, they spun little tops made of finely crafted birch as they crooned the Whiffenpoof. It was almost midnight and midtown was becoming a downtown filigree of lurching bodies, bent on finding their ways   and means of a short snooze till Starbuck time shook them once again. Blackening cedars set themselves against the limelighting stars, ghoulish figures startling just as many children as possible, given that most kids had been innoculated against all strains of startlization. It was an average wonderful evening, though one that would end in high-sea drama as a ship of fools careened into the crumbling concrete of High Street. Various manias would rise to the top of the poop deck and waltz with the few phobias left. And nobody cared. Not even the loop-de-loops of Old Town or the gaga Zsa Zsa's with their plunging drecklines. As always, there was Mr. and Mrs. O-Sole-Mio, and what a beautiful sunny day they suggested. With a shuffle-off-to-Buffalo bravado, holding each other's hand and vowing fidelity, *It's in your face, your face*, they sang, as though there would be nothing brighter than the next tomorrow. And tomorrow and tomorrow would be–surprise!– their twin melancholies. Melvin knew it, Kurt too. *So screw it*, a few skeptics muttered. But once begun, the lampooning would need to be seen through to the end. Whenever that could be safely predicted. Meanwhile, sunken treasure chests were retrieved from the deep, only to be found empty, though a few stylish remnants of the more stalwart fools were happily recovered. It is with this bounty that the wise can feel a little smug and ovine. Imagine what the feelish fool, that is, the foolish feel.

LE POINT DE VUE

A universal
view:
an object with a hole
l'objet avec le trou
is highly
desirable désirable atractiva atrativo
imagine a hole
without object mikpunt res obujekuto
le trou sans l'objet
how much more
désirable
aanlokkelijk nozomashii
agujero
cavus
ho-ru
hole
O
hål
furo
groef
depth without restriction
just enough resistance
accessible nocturnally diurnally
silent silencieuse stilzwijgend

or crying
sho-ro
O

AUTOBIEFFIGY

Four arms   four legs four each of eyes & ears
  (the better to see you with, my dear, & hear your huffing & puffing)
Two mouths: refusing to shut refusing to shut
Dentition: sixty-four canines all sharper than—thankfully!—a serpent's
Nose: one—but crackerjack! can quickly sniff out stench (mendacity
too)
Belly: two (for double the fire) Guts: lots (two little two large)
Four lungs—for taking a deep breath (& another another another)
Frontal lobes: two (for more frontal attacks on comings & goings)
Occipital: two (ensures not missing one thing or another)
Temporal: two (for keen hearing of cats, always hot on the roof)
Parietal: two (helps me manipulate my words)
Cerebellum: two—good when balance is wished-for (very occasional)
Four each of elbows & wrists ankles & knees (greater kinesis)
Vagina & breasts: for all impractical purposes, none
Personality: slightly split Rationality: fit Rascality: even fitter
Middle finger: four (in case there's any doubt)
Two hearts: one intact one slightly bleeding
Two third eyes (the better to leave you with)
There, I've sung—and maybe hung [make that *hanged*]—myself

VI. THEN ALL SMILES STOPPED

I gave commands;
Then all smiles stopped together.
Robert Browning
"My Last Duchess"

DOG DAYS

For a woman whose daughter
was killed by a boyfriend

Orange peels   tea leaves   eggshells   murder.
One more morning. The usual, the common.
No buffer makes a difference: sea   sun
geraniums in a windowbox   the dog's
warm weight at the foot of my bed. And Holly.
Her calls every morning, every night.

All stars seem biting now, the night
moon clawlike, or beefy. Since the murder.
Christmas trampled over grief. Even the holly
berries hurt, their red too fierce. The common
denominator for things I see is red—dog's
collar   apples in a bowl   a steak   the sun

growling into dusk   poppies. The sun-
shine used to quicken images and night
seemed a safe pocket to dream in. The dog-
star was a pure point of light. Then murder.
The twist on everything. I know common-
place kindnesses—warm bread   Holly's

casseroles   invitations out   Holly-
wood high-toned comfort   my son's
advice—should help to reinvent me. Common
sense says it should. But I read of night-
hawks everywhere, who track and murder
and murder tracks my head. I study the dog-

eared pages of their lives, over and over, with dogged
attempts to understand. Understand. Holly
tells me my daughter was always at risk, murder's
the pulse of city life. She says my son
is here, a blessing, and I don't suffer from night-
mares. No, just chronic hatred. In common,

maybe, with murderers. No, I'm not of their common-
wealth, so what do I do with this hate in the dog
days of another summer and the base nights
born from them? It doesn't matter. What Holly
says. Orange peels   tea leaves   the sun's
burning. Eggshells   a slapping sea   murder.

Common freight of every day. And Holly,
who dogs my steps. In the garden tonight the sun-
flowers look burly, roses bloody. Something's murdered.

TESTIMONY

Please raise your right hand

> She lifted a hook
> with an aging contraption—
> hooks gears springs
> *"Twenty years ago in California*
> *I was attacked…"*

Please raise your right hand
> She pointed
> *"… with a hatchet…*
> *my face, chest, stomach…"*
> he stared

> *"… eight times…"*
> he stared without expression
Please raise your right hook

PAN KETTLE PILLOW
U.S.A. *accidental fall down stairs* 2001
  beating... smothering 2006

Killed
by nephew and friends
the 84-year-old woman

After doting on the nephew
dipping into savings to support him
killed
in her kitchen

Killed
then positioned
at the bottom of stairs
to look as though
she'd fallen

Beaten, smothered
with a cast iron
frying pan and kettle
a pillow

Five years to find
she hadn't fallen
but was killed

LESS THAN EVER AFTER

I. USA 1994

The long ordeal of the sisters was made worse
because they could find no ally.

Stoop-shouldered   handcuffed   eyes downcast
he shuffled past his neighbors
He looked harmless

Everyone knew
they lived with a monster
three daughters who were fine
when their father was sober
Many days in a week he came home
drunk, threw the dog against a wall

Police silenced the girls' pleas:
Just disappear on weekends
Go back on Monday when he's sober

People knew
and they ignored it
said the youngest daughter
With the oldest, he fathered two babies
killing both at birth
burying one in the coal bin
one in the yard
He thought he'd never get caught
He looked harmless... for twenty-seven years

II. Austria 2008

I was born to rape, and I held myself back
for a relatively long time. I could have behaved
a lot worse than locking up my daughter.

jacquelyn shah
129

Once upon a time a king lured his daughter
to the basement of his man's-home-is-his-castle
led her through a labyrinth with low ceilings
to a padded cell.

He handcuffed and sedated her
with an ether-soaked towel. Against her will
he lay her down to father seven children.
He threatened electric shocks
gas, should she try to leave.

And so they stayed, daughter, children in the dungeon.
Unhappily, but not ever after... just twenty-four years.

MICKEY'S PANTS
Une souris verte file parmi la mousse
                              Apollinaire

Yes, it sneaks through the moss
mouse so sick it's turned green
squeaks through the moss, green
mouse in red pants, white gloves
mouse over-dosed on chocolate
mousse—is she just plain crazy?
Mickey's buttoned pants, the gloves—
will they make a difference
for une souris verte dans la mousse?

With this barely discernible squeak
you might think *no*
Red pants won't matter
nor the ball of a head, bright-eyed
smiley-faced, slicky and Mickey-like
Pipsqueakish, cette souris
without any cannon, without any balls
no virilities, nothing
but megaphone, useless
to broadcast some chicken-shit
scream, in a world ever-lost, o world…
and still, une souris verte
avec pantalon rouge
dreams of a scream as she sneaks and squeaks
and eats more mousse

ONE SHORT

Sadistic slayings
shocked Moscow
Russia 2007

For me, a life without murder
is like a life without food for you
he confessed

Luring his victims, many
homeless alcoholic elderly
with a bottle of vodka
Join me, he'd say
in mourning the death
of my dog

After getting them drunk
he'd hit them
multiple times
with a hammer
shattering skulls
throwing bodies
into a pit

He tallied his killings
on the 64 squares
of a chessboard
recording 63
one short of his goal

DIVERTIMENTO
Cape Cod, 2012

So little language needed for the music of a day
July, a sunny morning   birds   flowers
singing, singing out   come out
come into light air water   come without
a word   no tools but fingers for the day
to dig in sand   eat a clam   catch a head
or tail of thrill or quiet   turn a page
shade the eyes against the glare and glum
intruders   that say and say and say—
stay home and burrow into anything
but calm   while a razor threatens thin
illusions and a ripping thought begins
to cut across the lightest day with
bottom-heavy words words words…
take out a flute   a fan   a bubble-wand
pipe wave blow away the stiff corrupted
letters   huddling and conspiring
in rah-rah packs   pack up   get out   go singing
singing into light without a word
into light   without a word…

TOUGH

Woman, 112, too tough
for would-be burglar...
Girl, 16, hangs self
one year after rape...
USA: Michigan, Wisconsin
August 6, 1994

Five feet tall
112 years old—
she grabbed him
clawed his crotch
when he tried to rip her off

Gnarled fingers squeezed
He yelped   struggled
broke away and fled

I don't hate the man, she said
don't hate nobody

*   *   *   *   *   *   *

After the rape
she showered
three, four times a day
changing her clothes
at least three times

Just before her sixteenth birthday
in the woods behind her home
she hanged herself

... he killed her...
her mother said
it just took her a year to die

WRONG

The video is shaky, but
the brutality is clear.
                    Iraq 2007

A braying mob of men
drags a slender girl
in a headlock

On the ground
in fetal position
she covers her head
with her hands

Kicks   rocks…
then victorious shouts
from the men

Slam!
A concrete block
on the back
of her head
Blood oozes
She stops moving

She had loved a boy
from the wrong religion

A MOVING MASS
The act of the convict
has destroyed a life...
      India 2007

When jilted, he threatened to kill
then walked up and threw the acid

I screamed, writhed in pain...
then lost consciousness
  said the disfigured woman

The convict offered
to marry his victim

This person has pushed me
into a living hell
  said the blind woman

The convict offered again
to marry his victim,
seeking a lesser sentence

The judge:
. . . overzealous lover...
who reduced her to nothing
but a moving mass
of bones
and flesh

EVERYTHING
I love you, he told the woman…
Spain 2007

On TV he fell to his knees
cried and begged her
his estranged girl friend
offered her a ring

*I love you. You only live once
as you told me*, he said
*I want you to marry me
You are everything to me*
he pleaded, voice breaking

Face to face with him
this man
who had beaten her
for years
No, she would not
reconcile *No,
not in any way*

Four days later
she was found
in an elevator
throat slashed

WE WILL NOT STOP THEM

*This practice has been passed down
generation after generation, so it is natural.*

Egypt 2007

Seething, the men were seething...
a girl was dead

For centuries the practice persisted—
circumcision by doctor barber
or whoever else in the village
would put a girl to sleep
cut out her clitoris

*It assures chastity
It prevents homosexuality
It preserves family honor*
say the imams, in their mosques
Genital mutilation is good

The men were seething...
the clinic was closed
a ban on all genital cutting
imposed by the health minister

*Don't criticize the practice
of our fathers, and forefathers
It is natural to circumcise a daughter*
    says one imam

*Even if the state doesn't like it
we will circumcise the girls!*
    cries a village elder

They will not stop us!
    a man on the street shouts
They will not stop us!

—Q-SELF, JADING

Soul, self; come, poor Jackself, I do advise
You, jaded, let be; call off thought awhile…
                        Gerard Manley Hopkins

call it off   can you call it off   all dog thought
digging digging for bone   wetting your night brain
scratching your me-infested-me-infested hide
thought that pulls choke-collar-wise
till pop-eyed you're dog done   made dog   made dog again
and still boneless   still going on   look how you go on
cobbling some kind of something out of something
that grinds up your middle of the night
aren't you tired of it?
what is it   what is this Q of you you can't get over
get over it   this Q this quixotic you that blacktops over the soft self
and skates   back and forth   back and forth   back and forth
rating the world   berating the world and its scoring scoring
corrugated overrated backsliding world   horror of porn and war
cankering worms   call it off   this whirring of your won't-let-go
this diggery doggery mad-dog frothing at the mouth   useless foam of a
no
no-I-can't   when murdering is the loudest whirring
and night words cramp and crystal the mind
Q-infested-you-infested   bitten cur   kenneled in words
too damned faithful dog brain jading jading jading
whatever remains of your bitten-up soft-self…

NO

I will not go down to the river today
bending my way through brush
alone in the woods

I won't spread out on a beach
alone   where waves wash up needles
and dross

I won't walk out at night
into the darkness
darkness of never-come-back

I won't go buy and buy and buy
or swoon or suckle or kneel
I won't wear lace or velvet or silk
down to my ankles
up to my groin

I will never serve again
It's shattered—that platter
and the shards are gone

A father's tongue was thrust in the mouth
and sticks in the mouth forever, my mouth

I won't go down
to the river today
or down
in the woods of a world never mine
won't linger alone
won't bend
or serve
or kneel
or wink
at the darkness of fathers

CODAS

I PLEDGE ALLEGIANCE

to the night-blue field of my eyes
forever starless
my own unchangeable stripes
all morning-red
the indivisibility of my dissident heart
intact
despite its tangled web of hair-
line cracks   my embouchure
my cranky tone and home-grown stone
where there's never a son-of-a-bitch on the prowl

I pledge allegiance to all that swings
through my head   a monkey
telling me to mind the craters
that complicate a smooth and easy moon-self
hanging on like everyone

I pledge allegiance to maybe one more dawn
before a last gleaming
and to the ice cream cone you loved last night
and to the flavor of my own I-will-be-
quixotic-and-alone
within a cold gray brain-
space   the only place
to plumb   and play

PERFECT

I wish my deepest loving had as object
someone—Mother, Durga, Mary
Jesus, Thomas, Richard, Harry,
a human peerless, god or goddess perfect.
But every time I thought there was a prospect
(charming, steadfast, smart, extraordinary)
he turned out merciless, or mercenary.
Or (I knew why!), she was someone's reject.
So I proposed and I accepted, stroll
the aisle to plight my troth. *I do, I do.*
A veil is lifted, and with heart, head, soul
aflame, I kiss the air, bells clang on cue,
I shield my eyes from rice, and muse, distrustfully—
what discord is in store for me and me?

SWAN SONG: PREPOSTEROUS SONNETS FOR THE LETTER S

Even the mute swan, the least vocal species, often hisses,
making soft snoring sounds, or grunts sharply.

Hiss!   like a swan   enter queenly
            go slither   rather than glide
  embellishing S   look towards *serenely*
            echo   echo   side to side
one round to south   one to the north
            despoiling the channels with bilk
slippery   squiggling   back & forth
            schizoid   scissoring   snake in silk
sequacious   dextrous   Sew!
            stitch every sentence   sentence each stitch
to simply the *O*
            paired   impaired   gore self-pared from each
of the *O's*   Pen, swim in the squall of earth
            death be rounded with a little birth

Arise from ashes   to jeu d'esprit
            on lake of grunt & snore   Jet! Jet!
through jetsam hurled at See
            in cloud of feathers   asp attired in net
lob the juju   calque of jingle
            bob for snap   scrunching brow   go lunch
on smelt   then spit   swindle
            arch & archer   arrow-bound for finch
  [that destroyer of seeds of weeds—when
   you are weed   you are weed   you are weed]
Janus with a bipolarity
            of faces faces down & up   an eight
disfigured   the contrariety
            of endings & beginnings, your estate
Pen, fix the cob!   as Ashtoreth
      or Ardhanariswara   SSSS your shibboleth

FOOTNOTE

On my foot I write a note
    so it knows where not to go

knows to flee simoom
    find its fettle & thrive

With hope, it always understands
    pogonology & predator

I write by day   deliver nightly
    as foot begins to find its play   hop-

scotching tens & tens
    in its drawing-room   alone

Polyglottally, I write & sign it
    Eldritch, ever yours

WHAT TO DO WITH RED
—COLOR OF EXTREMES—

Fire Blood Passion Good Fortune Strength Power Energy Anger Daring Danger Warning War Creativity

NOTES FOR "Broken Jaw: A Cento"

The *cento* (from the Latin for *patchwork*) is a poetic form made up of lines from poems by other poets. The lines in "Broken Jaw: a Cento" are borrowed from:

Little by little the idea of the true way returned to me.
John Ashbery, "Wakefulness"

I think I did right to go out alone—
Mary Oliver, "The Kitten"

but salvation here? What about the rattle of sticks,
Wallace Stevens, "Parochial Theme"

stasis in darkness?
Sylvia Plath, "Ariel"

As a dare-gale skylark scanted in a dull cage
Gerard Manley Hopins, "The Caged Skylark"

I twist last year into a knot of old headlines
Adrienne Rich, "The Phenomenology of Anger"

and break onetwothreefourfive pigeonsjustlikethat.
e. e. cummings, "Buffalo Bill's"

This is the Sovereign Anguish!
Emily Dickinson, #167

This broken jaw of our lost kingdoms,
T. S. Eliot, "The Hollow Men"

which cannot be imposed on the unwilling victim,
"Cynthia Macdonald, "Objets D'Art"

parched my yearning, and a tuft of cellophane
James Tate, "City at Night"

broke into brand new things.
Rae Armantrout, "Accounts"

So I say to the worm, Hey, Puke Head, you're wearing my
Russell Edson, "The Eternal Worm"

shed snakeskin in the history of politeness.
Marianne Moore, "Marriage"

O for a beaker full of the warm South
John Keats, "Ode to a Nightingale"

and her teacup full of dark brown tears.
Elizabeth Bishop, "Sestina"

With those clear drops, which start like sacred dew
Percy Shelley, "Epipsychidion"

I have gone out, a possessed witch,
Anne Sexton, "Her Kind"

my heart in passion, and my head on rhymes.
Lord Byron, Don Juan, Canto 1, Stanza 217

Before me lies a mass of shapeless days.
Amy Lowell, "A Blockhead"

They set up a noise like crickets,
William Butler Yeats, "The Cap and Bells"

turning modest lodging into wraparound tropics.
Alice Fulton, "A Union House"

I remember the quick, nervous bird of your love
Billy Collins, "Paradelle for Susan"

always perched on the thinnest highest branch.
"   "

I believe reality is approximately 65% if,
Dean Young, "Belief in Magic"

with ribbons and bibbons on every side,
Edward Lear, "The Quangle Wangle's Hat"

and the too much of my speaking.
Paul Celan, "Below"